MUSIC
THROUGH
THE
AGES

IWO AND PAMELA ZALUSKI

YOUNG LIBRARY

Contents

First published in 1994 by
Young Library Ltd, 3 The Old Brushworks, 56 Pickwick Road, Corsham, Wiltshire SN13 9BX

© Copyright 1994 Young Library Ltd
All rights reserved

ISBN 1 85429 037 1
Printed and bound in Hong Kong

Prelude

What is music anyway? What is it for? Something to sing? Something to dance to? Something to cheer us when we are feeling fed up? A background noise while doing homework?

Yes. All of these things — and more. Music is the most powerful of all the arts. Apart from giving pleasure, its magic can calm the wildest tearaway, turn a pacifist into a warrior, and be a companion to lovers everywhere!

There are not many magic potions that can do all these things.

So what are the ingredients that make up this remarkable elixir?

Although musicians throughout the ages have added their own herbs and spices, there are three basic ingredients: melody, rhythm, and harmony. At least one of these must be present in any musical concoction. Words are an optional extra.

In this book we will see how the magic of music became part of our lives, ever since a primitive ancestor beat out a rhythm on a hollow log, and a bored shepherd played his first tune on a reed pipe . . .

How it all started

In the beginning, music was used mainly for praising gods, celebrating births and deaths, whipping up frenzy for war, sounding warnings of danger, and as hunting and work chants. It was also made purely for enjoyment. To people living a hard and uncomfortable life, singing and dancing to music was one of the few pleasures always available.

The earliest music was very primitive. It was made by beating out rhythms on a drum made of an animal skin stretched over a hollow trunk; plucking the string on a hunting bow; rattling seeds in gourds; blowing flutes made of reeds and hollowed-out bones; playing trumpets made from cattle horns and conch shells; scraping notched bones with a stick. Chanting, clapping, and whistling needed no equipment.

Ancient cave drawings show people playing reed pipes and drums.

It is impossible for us to know what the music of the ancient world actually sounded like. There was no notation until the Middle Ages, and recording was invented only at the end of the nineteenth century. All we have are history books; unfortunately they neither sing nor play instruments!

The Chinese were the first to make a study of music, which was used for worship and state functions. A music book of 1100 B.C. showed that they had orchestras which included giant drums, bells, gongs, trumpets, flutes, pan pipes, and a form of guitar. In the fifth century B.C. Confucius published a song book.

The Chinese arranged a system of 5 notes within an octave: the first known scale. Instead of a letter, each note had a

⬇ **Pythagoras discovered the idea of a scale of intervals between notes. This medieval drawing shows how the theory relates to the size of bells.**

PYTACORA

ÉVOLUTION DES INSTRUMENTS DE MUSIQUE.
1. Les instruments de musique chez les anciens Égyptiens et Hébreux.

VÉRITABLE EXTRAIT DE VIANDE LIEBIG.

⬆ **An array of musical instruments used by ancient Egyptians and Hebrews**

name: G was called The Emperor; A, The Prime Minister; B, The Loyal Subjects; D, Affairs of State; E, Mirror of the World. The next note was 'The Emperor' an octave higher.

This scale, called the pentatonic scale, is still used in China and parts of Africa, and features in Scottish folk music and Negro spirituals.

The Bible describes how the Israelites praised God with 'trumpets, harps, lyres, drums, dancing, cymbals, and flutes'. The Book of Genesis tells how Jubal invented the harp and the flute. Silver trumpets sent messages in the wilderness, and Joshua miraculously demolished the walls of Jericho with seven trumpets made of rams' horns.

David, composer of the Psalms, the first songs of praise, was the greatest musician in the Old Testament. He soothed King Saul's temper tantrums with his playing on the harp.

In ancient Egypt, music and dancing were used in all religious ceremonies. Hieroglyphs show musicians with lutes, harps, double flutes, and lyres. Two trumpets were found in Tutankhamun's tomb, which are still playable today.

To the Babylonians music was very important. As clapping and dancing were featured prominently, the music was obviously rhythmic. The instruments were similar to those of the Israelites, who

exchanged musical ideas with them during their captivity in Babylon.

In India, music was regarded as a gift from the gods. Religious chants, called vedas, had melodies with no set rhythm. They were sung from memory, and passed down the generations by ear. Among early instruments was the vina, a 7-stringed guitar-like instrument with hollow gourds attached to give resonance.

The Greek god of music was Apollo. He is often portrayed with a lyre. Under his inspiration, the Greeks developed music where the Chinese left off. In the sixth century B.C. the mathematician Pythagoras analysed music. He used science to determine the pitch of notes, and worked out the principle of tones and semi-tones.

Pythagoras divided the octave into the 8-note scale used throughout the world today. He worked out alternative scales, which are called modes. These are still used for special effects. The best known is the Aeolian Mode, the basis for the minor key.

The Greeks used music as an art form, to be enjoyed and admired. The philosopher Plato wrote that music should ennoble and soothe. They united spoken poetry with music. To the Greeks, who were great poets and dramatists, words were the most important; the music had to fit the rhythm of the words.

Greek art shows lyres, flutes, tambourines, pan pipes (named after the god Pan), and castanets. The Pythian Games were musical competitions in praise of Apollo.

The epic poet Homer sang his poems. In his *Odyssey* he introduced the Sirens — maidens who sang so beautifully that they lured sailors to their doom. Achilles, the hero of Homer's *Iliad*, played the lyre. So did Orpheus, favourite Greek hero, who appears in many operas.

Greek music declined when Greece was conquered by Rome. To the Romans music was only for relaxation, dancing, and orgies. The high Greek ideals were all but lost, and music took a backward step, from which it took several centuries to recover.

➤ **Pan was the Greek god of forests, pastures, flocks, and shepherds. He is usually shown as a goat-legged man playing the pipes which are named after him.**

2

More than one tune at a time

The ingredients of ancient music were melody and rhythm — not necessarily at the same time. There were chants with no beat, and drumming with no tune; in some parts of the world this still happens.

During the first fifteen centuries A.D. changes took place in European music which affected the whole world.

Music became part of Christian ceremonies. The ancient Jewish temple tradition and Greek modes were kept going in monasteries by monks chanting psalms and songs of praise. By 600 A.D. Christian music, and its modes, had been standardized by Bishop Ambrose of Milan and Pope Gregory I.

The Ambrosian and Gregorian chants, now called plainsong, were sung in Latin, and used notation for the first time. Plainsong was written on a stave of four lines, with the notes represented by small black squares and diamonds. There was no time signature, as plainsong had no beat. The oldest manuscripts of plainsong date back to the ninth century.

▶ **Music notation was invented by Guido d'Arezzo a thousand years ago. This memory aid, which includes the original four-line stave shown on the wrist, might have been drawn by him.**

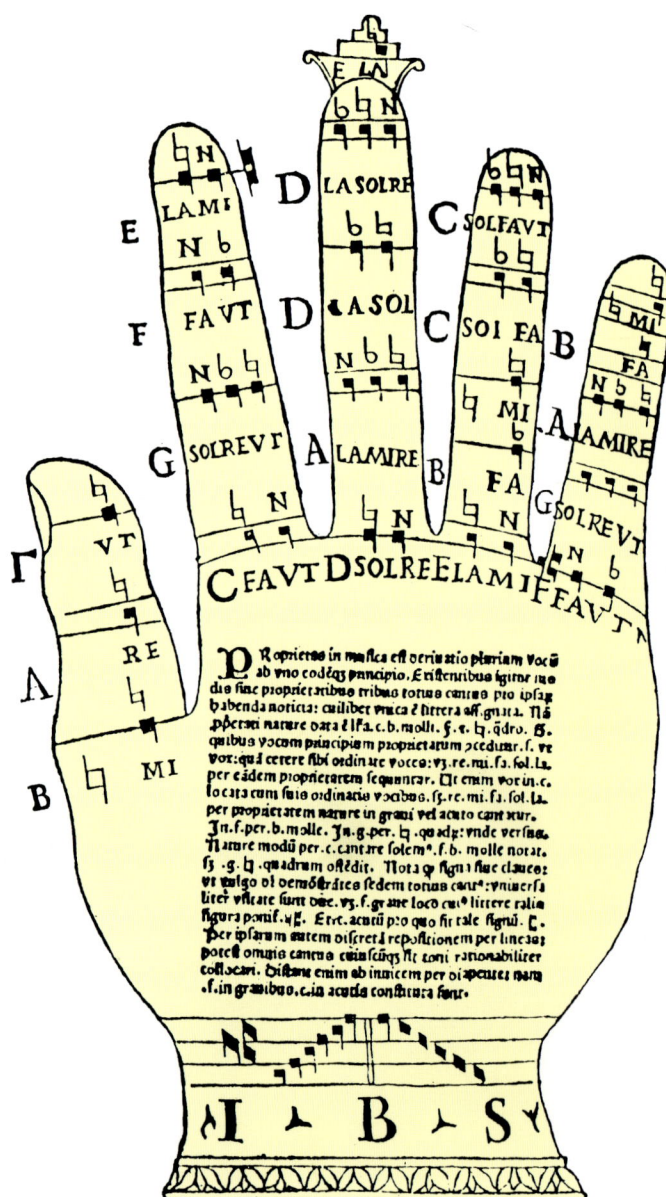

🔺 **Medieval street bands were called waits. This English wait consists of pipe and tabor, viol, shawm, lute, and oboe.**

Plainsong is still used in the Roman Catholic church. Because of notation, it is possible to sing it as it was written fifteen centuries ago. It is usually chanted without accompaniment, although sometimes an organ is added. The Greek modes and lack of rhythm give plainsong a strangely mystical sound.

In about A.D. 1000, the French-born Italian monk Guido d'Arezzo invented the five-line stave, and the notation that is used world-wide to this day.

In the fifteenth century monks experimented by singing the same tune but at different intervals by different voices (one voice echoing another). These devices were called canons and rounds — much used by children today. They also discovered the beautiful effect of using a second tune to weave in and out of the main tune.

By singing two tunes at the same time the monks discovered the most important musical phenomenon of all — polyphony (in Greek, *poly* means many and *phonos* means sound). The tunes did not always fit, but the monks became expert at counterpoint — the art of making tunes fit.

The double round, 'Sumer is Icumen In' (Summer is a-coming in), written by monks in Reading in the thirteenth century, is the oldest piece of polyphonic music in existence. Apart from the four voices of a normal round, it also has a two-voice bass part repeating a droning accompaniment throughout.

Most polyphonic music was written for four, five, or six voices. The English composer Thomas Tallis (about 1505-1585), wrote a Latin motet (an early type of hymn) called 'Spem in Alium' for forty separate voices!

In the Middle Ages a musician could not earn a living unless he was employed by a court or church as a singer, player, or

A 19th-century painting of medieval minstrels arriving at a castle.

This is a portrait of Monteverdi, who wrote the very first opera, *Orfeo*, performed in 1607. The book in which this portrait appears with various 17th-century instruments was specially prepared for his funeral.

composer. Women were not admitted, and choirs used boys' voices instead of women's.

Talented entertainers earned money as wandering singers, accompanying themselves on lutes or guitars. They were called troubadours in France, minnesingers in Germany, and minstrels in England. They sang anything from love songs to epic ballads of adventure and romance. A famous minstrel called Blondel sang around Europe until he found his master — King Richard the Lion-Heart — imprisoned in a castle.

In Italy polyphony was growing faster than in England. By the end of the sixteenth century Italy led the world in music. Composers were needed to write masses and other religious music for Catholic ser-

vices. The greatest was Giovanni Palestrina (1525-94). Many musicians copied his rich style, including Claudio Monteverdi (1567-1643). Monteverdi wrote not only religious music but the first opera.

An opera is a sung play. Monteverdi's opera *Orfeo* (Orpheus) was the first in a long Italian operatic tradition. Renowned for their fine voices, Italians have led the world in opera to this day.

They also invented madrigals — polyphonic songs to be sung for fun. In Tudor times madrigals were very fashionable in England.

So by the middle of the seventeenth century the third basic ingredient of music — harmony — had been added to melody and rhythm.

3

The well-tempered orchestras of the Baroque era

In the seventeenth century music was enriched by the addition of instruments to the voices. Recorders, viols, oboes, trumpets, organ, and keyboards, together with voices, produced a rich tapestry of sound which became known as 'baroque'.

At this time the orchestra came into its own, but instruments were rough and out of tune. Italian craftsmen began to build instruments scientifically, applying the laws of physics.

The thin-toned viols were replaced by the richer violin, viola, violincello, and double bass. Niccolò Amati (1596-1684) and his pupil Antonio Stradivari (1644-1737) made superb violins. The secret lay in the

◀ **Until the invention of electricity, organs had to be pumped by the assistant, like this very early organ used by a travelling performer.**

↑ A 19th-century painting showing the violin-maker Stradivari in his workshop at Cremona, Italy.

varnish; unfortunately, this secret died with the makers. The instruments improved with age, and today a Stradivarius is the best violin that money can buy.

Early keyboards like harpsichords and virginals plucked the strings. Therefore they only played at one volume no matter how hard the keys were struck. In 1710 Bartolomeo Cristofori invented the piano by producing a harpsichord which could play softly (in Italian, *piano*) and loudly (*forte*). The 'pianoforte' used little hammers to hit the strings instead of quills to pluck them.

The Germans also built fine instruments. Gottfried Silbermann (1683-1753) built magnificent organs and the first German piano. Woodwind instruments were built scientifically, with the holes in just the right places so that the notes could play in tune. At the end of the seventeenth century Johann Denner (1655-1707) invented the clarinet.

This attention to pitch culminated in *The Well-Tempered Clavier* (often called *The 48*) by Johann Sebastian Bach (1685-1750). Bach is regarded by many as the greatest musician ever. Claviers (keyboard instruments) were badly tuned, and musicians with fine hearing found that if they were in tune in one key, they sounded out of tune in another. At first no one minded, as music was usually played in easy keys. Bach insisted on fine tuning, or 'tempering', so that the twelve semitones were in perfect tune. *The 48* consists of two sets of preludes and fugues, covering every key — 12 major and 12 minor.

The growth of the orchestra led to the next stage of harmony. Instead of several tunes being played together, composers wrote tunes with 'blocks' of fitting notes as accompaniments. These became known as chords. Clavier music was often a bass line with coded numbers underneath, from which players worked out the chords in their own way, as guitar chords are written in under the stave today. So clavier players became what pianists are today — solo players or accompanists.

Domenico Alberti (1710-40) developed a left-hand accompaniment of flowing patterns made up of the notes of the chord. This device kept the music moving instead of plodding. The 'Alberti bass' was copied by most composers at the time.

Baroque music was grand and graceful, ornate and complex. Notes were 'decorated' by many trills and turns, especially by singers wishing to show off their techniques.

Among the leading baroque composers at this time were Jean-Baptiste Lully (1632-87) and Jean-Phillippe Rameau (1683-1764) in France; Alessandro Scarlatti (1660-1725) and Antonio Vivaldi (1678-1741), who wrote *The Four Seasons*, in Italy; Henry Purcell (1659-95) in England, and Johann Sebastian Bach (1685-1750) in Germany.

Bach wrote a tremendous amount of music, especially for the church. Among the finest are the *Mass in B minor*, and the oratorio *St Matthew Passion*, the Easter story set to music, with different singers taking the leading parts. They are both very long and grand, feature solo singers, choir (boys and men only) and orchestra. Bach's music represents the most glorious achievements of the baroque period.

A picture of Vivaldi, the composer of *The Four Seasons*.

4

The birth of the classical symphony

The German princes in the seventeenth century employed a *Kappellmeister*. He took charge of the orchestra and composed music for special occasions — dance music for balls, and background music for summer evenings and banquets. Most baroque and classical music was written for such occasions.

The twelve German ruling princes, called Electors, were brought up to be musicians, and joined in the court music-making.

German-born George Frideric Handel (1685-1759) was *Kappellmeister* to the Elector of Hanover. Both later came to England, Handel to pursue a career as composer of operas and oratorios, the Elector to take the British throne as King George I.

During the first performance of Handel's oratorio *The Messiah*, George II, son of George I, was so excited by the 'Hallelujah Chorus' that he stood up. Out of politeness, the whole audience did the same. The tradition continues to this day.

In the eighteenth century, form became all-important. Music was composed according to the rules. Formal dances, such as minuets and gavottes, had to be learned. A popular musical form was the suite (in

Handel, England's greatest composer, was in fact German-born. He spent most of his life in England, and is buried in Westminster Abbey.

French, *suivre* means to follow). A set of four, five, or six dances followed on from each other. Each dance was called a 'movement'.

Operas were becoming popular, especially those about Greek mythology.

◄ By the beginning of the 18th century magnificent organs like this could be found in churches and cathedrals all over Europe.

▶ In this picture Mozart is seven years old. He is seated at the harpsichord, with his father on violin, and eleven-year-old sister Nannerl singing.

Christoph Gluck (1714-87) wrote many such operas in Paris and Vienna, including yet another one about Orpheus. 'Opera buffa', such as Mozart's *The Magic Flute*, were fashionable comedies, full of attractive, hummable tunes.

Operas opened with an 'overture', an orchestral piece to set the scene. It was always fast-slow-fast, and had nothing to do with the story; but some composers constructed the overtures from the best tunes of the opera — a foretaste of delights to come. Others just wrote orchestral overtures without the opera. So 'overture' came to mean any piece of fast-slow-fast orchestral music.

Like Handel, Johann Christian Bach (1735-82), son of J.S. Bach, lived in London. He separated the fast-slow-fast sections into three separate pieces, like the movements of a suite. This caused a new trend for writing concert pieces. Some composers added a dance movement, making a new, more complex 4-movement form.

An orchestra of 2 flutes, 2 oboes, 2 bassoons, 2 horns, and a complete string section was considered the best combination. The *Kappellmeister* to the Elector of the Palatinate, Johann Stamitz (1717-57), made his orchestra practise regularly on good instruments, and play in tune and

with feeling. His Mannheim orchestra was by far the best and most famous in Europe. He stood before his players, waving a stick to make sure they played exactly as he wished. Stamitz had invented conducting.

This new music — the suite of fast and slow movements — had a new name: the 'symphony' (in Greek, *sym* means together and *phonos* means sound). It told no story, and was not descriptive. It was pure, skilfully scored, concert music for listening to. The first movement was fast-moving, the second slow, the third a lighter dance, and the fourth a fast finale. The orchestra was called the symphony orchestra.

The symphonic formula is the same to this day — with added modifications.

When he was eight years old, Wolfgang Amadeus Mozart (1756-91) met J.C. Bach in London. Bach was very impressed with the boy's amazing talent, and played him some of his symphonies. Little Mozart promptly wrote two symphonies of his own. He went on to write over forty, including his 'Jupiter' symphony.

J.C. Bach invented the symphony. Mozart, with Joseph Haydn (1732-1809), who wrote 106, perfected it.

The Concerto is a symphony in three movements featuring a solo instrument, or group of instruments, with orchestra. Most are for piano or violin, and feature a 'cadenza', where the soloist improvises, showing off his (or her — women were now accepted) skills.

String quartets, for 2 violins, viola, and cello, were developed by Haydn. The slow movement of his 'Emperor' Quartet is now the German National Anthem. Mozart and Ludwig van Beethoven (1770-1827) both wrote many concertos and string quartets.

🔺 Beethoven's 'mind's ear' was so developed that he carried on writing even after he became completely deaf.

Sonatas (in Italian, *suonare* means to sound) were symphonies for solo keyboard or duet. J.C. Bach's brother, C.P.E. Bach (1714-1788), wrote seventy-seven of them. Domenico Scarlatti (1685-1757), son of Alessandro, wrote 545 hugely popular sonatas. Mozart wrote over forty.

Beethoven wrote in the classical style when young. However, his last piano sonatas and string quartets, born of the angry world of his own deafness, are dramatically creative. They are difficult to listen to, and require great concentration.

Beethoven raised the symphony to the highest musical form. He added soloists and chorus to the massive last movement of his 'Choral' Symphony — the magnificent 'Ode to Joy' — now the European Community anthem.

5

The romantic movement

The nineteenth century, a period of revolution and change, led to the 'romantic movement'. Bigger and better orchestras, more vivid imaginations, new concert halls, theatres, and music publishers, all gave new opportunities to composers. They wrote music that they wanted to write, rather than what an Elector required.

The word 'romantic' suggests love, but there is a wider meaning. Adventure, heroics, scenery, and tragedy all play a part. Romantic music told a story, painted a picture in sound, inspired calm, anger or love, expressed a composer's feelings.

Soaring violin melodies inspired love; brass and drums described storms and battles; languid piano pieces brought feelings of sadness; massive orchestral chords suggested tragedy; actions were depicted by rhythms.

Audiences closed their eyes, and the music transported them to magic lands of the imagination.

This did not happen suddenly.

Beethoven's 'Pastoral' Symphony describes the sounds of the countryside, including a thunderstorm. When composer Carl Weber (1786-1826) heard it, he was shocked. 'Mr Beethoven is now ripe for the madhouse!' he wrote.

⬆ **Paganini wrote such difficult violin music that people swore he was in league with the devil. A great showman, he encouraged this rumour!**

Twenty-three years later the French composer Hector Berlioz (1803-1869) wrote his 'Fantastic' (meaning Fantasy) Symphony. It is wildly imaginative, starting with a Dream of Love, and ending with the March to the Scaffold and a Witches' Sabbath! Berlioz was among the first to use

⬆ **Liszt was another genius and showman. These cartoons show the grandiloquent gestures he performed for the sake of his female admirers.**

'image'. With his good looks, long hair and flashy clothes, he would posture wildly while conducting his enormous orchestra. His epic opera *The Trojans* is so enormous that it was not produced until 1906!

The Hungarian Franz Liszt (1811-1886) was a superb pianist. As piano manufacturers were ever building new, improved models, the fashion among pianists was to show off their technique. Nothing pleased Liszt more than to display his incredible skill and handsome profile in front of admiring ladies, playing his extremely difficult *Hungarian Rhapsodies*.

Another leading romantic composer was the songwriter Franz Schubert (1797-1828),whose 'Unfinished' Symphony is classical in form, but romantic in feeling.

Felix Mendelssohn (1809-47), pictured the sea in his *Hebrides* overture, and wrote the *Wedding March* to Shakespeare's *A Midsummer Night's Dream*. His sister Fanny composed; in the nineteenth century the emancipation of women had begun. Robert Schumann (1810-1856) and his wife, Clara, each wrote a piano concerto full of rich, romantic melodies.

'Nationalism' in music was growing. Many nations were occupied by foreign powers, and music was an expression of independence.

Frederick Chopin (1810-1849), of French-Polish parentage, wrote some of the century's finest piano pieces, many based on Polish folk music.

The Czech composers Antonin Dvořák

> The Czech composer Dvořák went to America, where he wrote his immensely popular 'New World' Symphony because he was homesick for his native land.

> Schubert was so awestruck by Beethoven that he would sit in the same coffee house, but never plucked up the courage to speak to him.

(1841-1904), of 'New World' Symphony fame, and Bedrich Smetana (1824-1884), whose *Vltava* tells the story of Bohemia's biggest river, both longed for freedom from Austrian rule, and used Czech folk tunes.

Edvard Grieg (1843-1907), Norwegian composer of the most famous piano concerto of all, wrote music describing Norway's scenery and folk tales about trolls.

In Russia Alexander Borodin (1833-1887), Modest Mussorgsky (1839-81), and Nicolai Rimsky-Korsakov (1844-1908), wrote operas about Russian heroes and the mystic East. Ballet was becoming popular, and Peter Tchaikovsky (1840-93), the greatest ballet composer of all, wrote *The Nutcracker* and *The Sleeping Beauty*. Russia has led the world in ballet ever since. Jean Sibelius (1865-1957) was inspired by the myths and sagas of his native Finland, then occupied by Russia.

New musical forms came into being.

Symphonic poems are descriptive pieces for orchestra, many telling stories. Liszt wrote sixteen, including *Mazeppa*, the tale of a Ukrainian hero's adventures. Richard Strauss (1864-1949) wrote ten, including

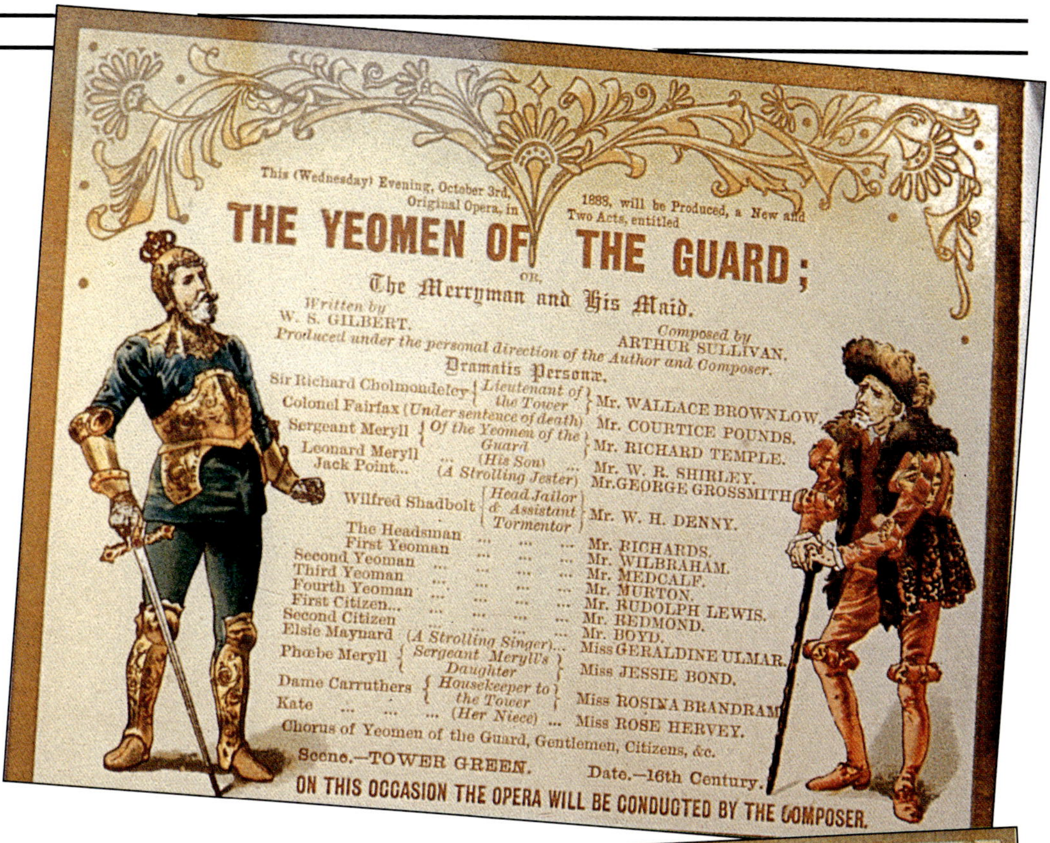

The theatre programme for one of Gilbert and Sullivan's comic operas. Never a day goes by without at least one being performed somewhere in the world.

This (Wednesday) Evening, October 3rd, 1888, will be Produced, a New and Original Opera, in Two Acts, entitled

THE YEOMEN OF THE GUARD;
OR,
The Merryman and His Maid.

Written by
W. S. GILBERT.

Composed by
ARTHUR SULLIVAN.

Produced under the personal direction of the Author and Composer.

Dramatis Personæ.

Sir Richard Cholmondeley	{Lieutenant of the Tower}	Mr. WALLACE BROWNLOW.
Colonel Fairfax	(Under sentence of death)	Mr. COURTICE POUNDS.
Sergeant Meryll	{Of the Yeomen of the Guard}	Mr. RICHARD TEMPLE.
Leonard Meryll	(His Son)	Mr. W. R. SHIRLEY.
Jack Point...	(A Strolling Jester)	Mr. GEORGE GROSSMITH.
Wilfred Shadbolt	{Head Jailor & Assistant Tormentor}	Mr. W. H. DENNY.
The Headsman.		
First Yeoman	...	Mr. RICHARDS.
Second Yeoman	...	Mr. WILBRAHAM.
Third Yeoman	...	Mr. MEDCALF.
Fourth Yeoman	...	Mr. MURTON.
First Citizen...	...	Mr. RUDOLPH LEWIS.
Second Citizen	...	Mr. REDMOND.
Elsie Maynard	(A Strolling Singer)...	Mr. BOYD.
Phœbe Meryll	{Sergeant Meryll's Daughter}	Miss GERALDINE ULMAR.
Dame Carruthers	{Housekeeper to the Tower}	Miss JESSIE BOND.
Kate	(Her Niece) ...	Miss ROSINA BRANDRAM.
		Miss ROSE HERVEY.

Chorus of Yeomen of the Guard, Gentlemen, Citizens, &c.

Scene.—TOWER GREEN.   Date.—16th Century.

ON THIS OCCASION THE OPERA WILL BE CONDUCTED BY THE COMPOSER.

The Scenery painted by Mr. HAWES CRAVEN (by permission of Mr. HENRY IRVING).
The Dresses designed by Mr. PERCY ANDERSON, and executed by Miss FISHER, Mdme. LEON, and M. BARTHE.   Wigs by CLARKSON.   The Dances arranged by Mr. JOHN D'AUBAN.
Musical Director ... Mr. FRANCOIS CELLIER.   Stage Manager ... Mr. W. H. SEYMOUR.

The Theatre is lighted entirely by Electricity.

NO FEES OF ANY KIND.

Box Office always open from 9 a.m. till 11 p.m.

Johann Strauss the Younger wrote more than 400 waltzes, including the famous *Blue Danube*. This picture shows his orchestra performing at a Viennese ball.

⬆ Wagner's cycle of operas, *The Ring of the Nibelung*, based on a Norse myth, takes 17 hours to perform. This illustration shows the goddess Freya's kidnap by giants Fasolt and Fafner.

⬆ **Mahler wrote ten enormous symphonies, including the *Symphony of a Thousand*, which requires up to 1000 musicians and singers to perform, and lasts one-and-a-half hours.**

1868) wrote popular and tuneful operas, including *William Tell*, whose overture is well known. The operas of Guiseppe Verdi (1813-1901) were grand spectacles, the most famous being *Aida*. Giacomo Puccini (1858-1924) composed *Turandot*, from which 'Nessun Dorma' is the most famous aria.

In France, Georges Bizet (1838-75) wrote *Carmen*, which includes the 'Toreador's Song'. Jacques Offenbach (1819-80) wrote light operas, the most famous being *Orpheus in the Underworld*, with its famous 'Can-Can'.

In England people flocked to the tuneful operettas of Gilbert and Sullivan, such as *The Mikado* and *The Pirates of Penzance*.

The biggest operas were those of Richard Wagner (1813-83). The four operas that make up *The Ring of the Nibelung*, altogether lasting seventeen hours, tell of the magic Rhinegold and the destruction of Valhalla. Wagner had a theatre specially built at Bayreuth, in Germany, to put on his operas.

The symphony became the most perfect musical form. Long and complex, symphonies require concentrated listening. Johannes Brahms (1833-97), composer of the famous 'Cradle Song', wrote four, and Anton Bruckner (1824-96) wrote eleven.

But it was Gustav Mahler (1860-1911) who topped everyone for sheer size. His Eighth Symphony lasts one-and-a-half hours, and requires up to a thousand performers including soloists, choruses, and an enormous orchestra.

Was this the end of the romantic era?

Also Sprach Zarathustra, about Man's struggle against Nature. Its dramatic opening is used as the music to NASA's space projects. Camille Saint-Saëns (1835-1921), composer of *Carnival of the Animals*, wrote four, including *Danse Macabre*, about a night-time ghost party in a graveyard!

Opera was becoming grander. A new style of singing, originating in Italy, was called *bel canto* (in Italian it means beautiful song). This entailed rigorous technical training, and is still essential to all opera singers today. Gioacchino Rossini (1792-

6

Experiments with scales

When the French composer Claude Debussy (1862-1918) heard an Indonesian Gamelan orchestra he was struck by the weird and wonderful sounds of the gongs and bells.

Like many composers towards the end of the nineteenth century, he was growing tired of sentimental romanticism, and was looking for new ideas. Gamelan music, with its peculiar 5-note scale, inspired him to experiment with other scales. He tried the Chinese pentatonic scale and the Greek modes, as well as the diatonic (major and minor) scales. Debussy invented the 7-note whole tone scale — from C to C without semitones. The result was a blurred sound, with no recognizable harmony or tune, which he liked.

His music reflected feelings and impressions, rather than direct descriptions. He once commented to an amazed girl friend that in his head he could hear the music of grass growing. But the music came from a feeling of tranquillity and love, as they relaxed in the park on a summer's day, with the sounds of children playing and insects buzzing.

Debussy's music, with its vague, rambling melodies and strangely beautiful harmonies, came to be called impressionism.

At first the public found these new sounds difficult. His publisher complained that in his orchestral piece, *Sirènes* (the Sirens who lured sailors to their doom), there was a women's chorus that sang to 'ah'. Where were the words? Debussy pointed out to the incredulous publisher that in this case women's voices were used as an orchestral instrument.

Debussy wrote a great deal of piano music, including the peaceful *Clair de Lune* (Moonlight) and the mysterious *La Cathédrale Engloutie*, describing a phantom cathedral emerging from a foggy sea. The tolling of bells and the monks' plainchant can be 'vaguely' heard in the music.

Impressionism, in both music and painting, was a particularly French phenomenon. Debussy's ideas were shared by Maurice Ravel (1875-1937). Ravel's famous *Bolero*, written for an 'exotic dancer', had nothing to do with impressionism; but his 'Sunrise' in the ballet *Daphnis et Chloé*, is one of the most spectacular pieces of impressionist music.

Impressionism was meant to be enjoyed as one would enjoy the sound of the sea, of birds singing, or even of a tap dripping.

There was another revolt against 'romantic sentimentality' at the turn of the

⬆ **Debussy's music is a mixture of dream and beautiful sounds. It is well illustrated by this stage setting for his descriptive piece, *Afternoon of a Faun*.**

century. The Austrian Arnold Schoenberg (1874-1951) began as a romantic, but it was an age of experiments. While Debussy was exploring alternative scales, Schoenberg used the 12-tone chromatic scale, consisting of every note from C to C.

The public were used to eight notes at a time, as they are to this day. Twelve notes of equal importance produced melodies and harmonies that sounded discordant and harsh to those who did not understand.

Schoenberg's music threw all rules out of the window and introduced new ones. The composer first arranged the twelve notes in a particular order, or 'series' for one instrument, or group of instruments, then developed this series to produce a melody line. He would do the same for other instruments. The construction is similar to the old polyphony, but the sounds do not harmonize in the accepted sense.

Schoenberg's ideas were copied and developed by his pupils Anton Webern (1883-1945), and Alban Berg (1885-1935). This music, to be listened to with the head rather than the heart, was called serialism.

Impressionism and serialism continue to influence composers to this day.

Music in the New World

The Americas are a melting pot of European, African, and Amerindian descent, and American music reflects this. In 1620 the religious Pilgrim Fathers settled in North America, and brought with them a tradition of hymn-singing. The first American composer was Johann Beissel (1690-1768), who wrote hymns.

At this time African slaves were brought to America. Their musical tradition contained two significant ingredients: rhythm, and improvisation (which means composing music on the spot).

The two cultures blended to produce the first truly American music: the Negro spiritual. This is a highly emotional and rhythmic religious song, sung by a soloist skilled in improvisation, accompanied by the chorus singing in harmony.

Spirituals evolved into the blues — the music of misery. To have the blues meant to be deeply depressed. Blues singing was emotional, and included sobbing, sighing, and crying, as well as 'bending' and decorating notes.

Pianos, guitars, and banjos were used as accompaniments. Pianists developed a bouncy, rhythmic style of solo playing called ragtime. Scott Joplin (1868-1917), composer of 'The Entertainer' was its greatest exponent.

Music in the European style was also being written. Edward Macdowell (1861-1908) was writing romantic piano music, and Mrs H.H.A. Beach (1867-1944), the wife of a New York doctor, was America's greatest woman composer.

Louis Gottschalk (1829-1869), a composer and pianist of French, Creole, and Jewish descent, stunned audiences with his brilliant blend of romantic, ragtime, and South American rhythms.

Two composers described the American way of life. Charles Ives (1874-1954) wrote *Fourth of July* and *Putnam's Camp*, which uses several orchestra groups playing different music at the same time to describe American 'razzmatazz'. The music of Aaron Copland (1900-90) includes the ballets *Rodeo*, *Billy the Kid* and *Appalachian Spring*.

In the nineteenth and early twentieth centuries, European immigrants brought their music to the New World. Among them were the adventurous Irish, whose lilting folk songs round Wild West camp fires were adapted to form what is known today as country and western music.

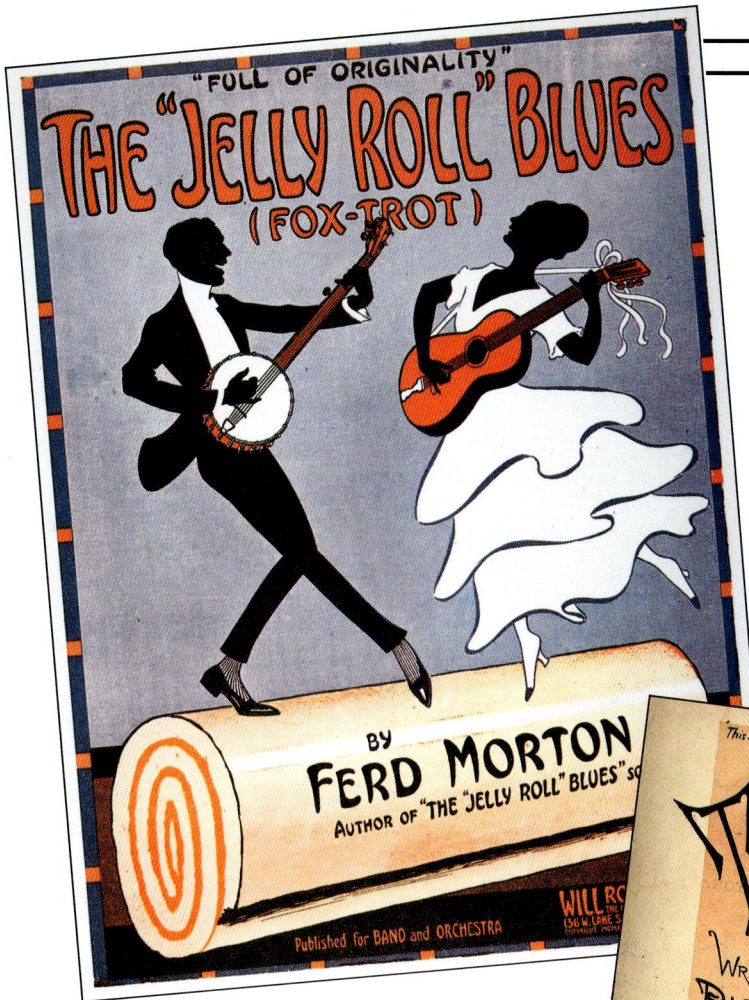

The "Jelly Roll" Blues (Fox-Trot)
"Full of Originality"
By Ferd Morton
Author of "The "Jelly Roll" Blues" Song
Published for Band and Orchestra

◆ This cover of a song-sheet expresses the exuberant ragtime and razzmatazz in America at the turn of the 20th century. The banjo and the guitar were favourite instruments with both black and white entertainers.

Ta-Ra-Ra-Boom-Der-Ay.
Written by Richard Morton.
Music Arranged by Angelo A. Asher
Lottie Collins's Greatest Creation.
Copyright, 1891. London, Charles Sheard & Co. Music Publishers & Printers, 192, High Holborn, W.C.

◆ In England Music Hall favourites such as TA-RA-RA-BOOM-DER-AY were published as sheet music, so that families and friends could sing the songs around the piano in their own homes.

⬆ **The Dodge City Cowboy Band of 1886 consists of brass, percussion, and at least 3 revolvers!**

Negroes adopted some of the settlers' instruments and added them to blues and ragtime. The result, originating in New Orleans, was called jazz. The first jazz bands consisted of a 'front line' of trumpet, clarinet, and trombone, and a 'rhythm section' of piano, guitar or banjo, and double bass. The music was always improvised around the tune. The result was highly emotional 'instant polyphony', with a strong beat. Trumpeter Louis Armstrong (1900-71) and pianist 'Fats' Waller (1904-

43) were two of jazz's greatest artists. Jazz was not considered respectable, and could only be heard in the bars of tough, inner city areas.

In the 1920s jazz caught on with European musicians, and a new 'white' jazz style called Dixieland emerged. Improvisation was not commonly practised by European musicians until they began copying the New Orleans sound.

Dixieland Jazz led to the first 'pop' music — the dance bands and big 'swing' bands

⬆ This photograph shows King Oliver kneeling with his trombone in front of his Creole Jazz Band. In the background is the young trumpeter Louis Armstrong.

▶ Elvis Presley, undisputed king of rock 'n' roll, died in 1977.

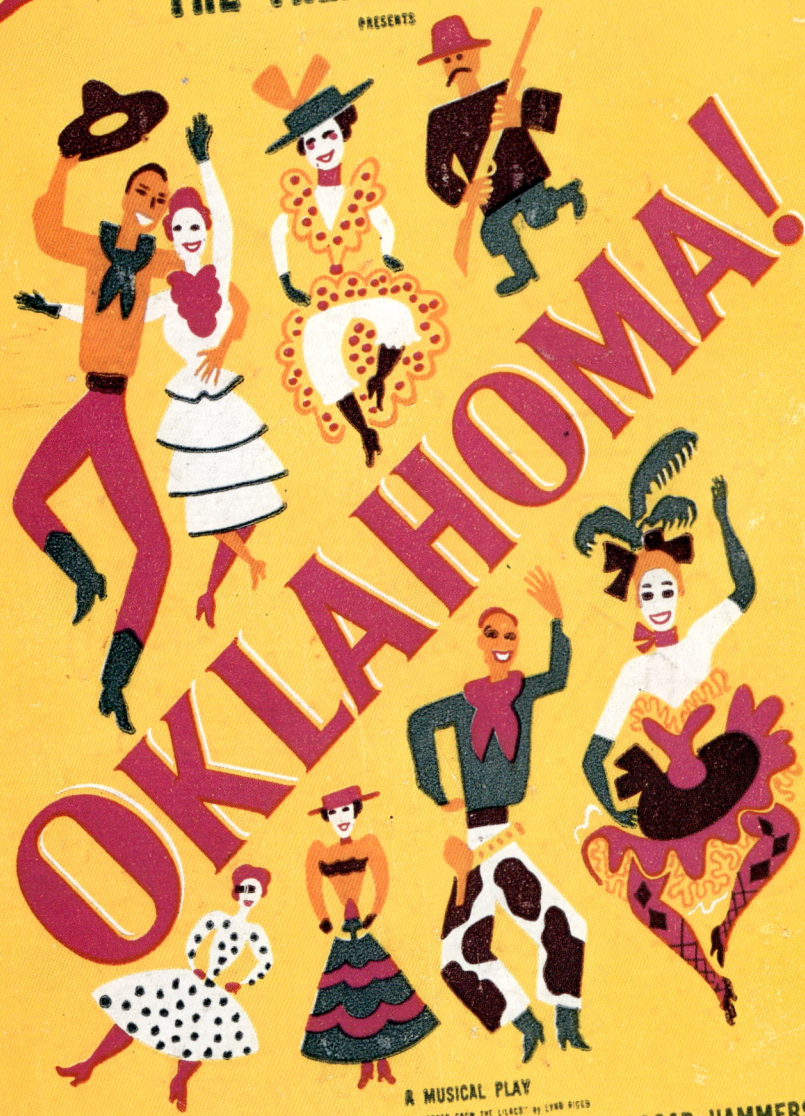

◀ Rodgers and Hammerstein was the most
successful partnership in the history of the
American musical. *Oklahoma* was their first
great hit.

of the 1930s. The 'front line' grew to
several trumpets, saxophones, and trom-
bones. The music, written as for a symphony orchestra, had spots for
improvisation. Among the greatest big
band leaders was Duke Ellington (1899-
1974).

Dance bands and big bands usually featured vocalists, and many of these, like
Frank Sinatra (born 1915), became solo
artists in their own right. In the 1950s the
'swing' style of the big bands was replaced
by the wilder rock 'n' roll, started by Bill
Haley and the Comets. The greatest rock
'n' roll performer was Elvis Presley (1935-
1977).

⬇ George Gershwin is one of America's
greatest composers. His famous *Rhapsody in
Blue* successfully combined jazz and classical
forms, as did his opera *Porgy and Bess*.

From the 1960s onwards, rock music has
been an ever-changing pageant of different styles, including the '60s', and Tamla
Motown. The 1960s songs of Beatles
Lennon and McCartney influence rock
composers to this day.

In jazz, the big bands led to small groups
playing in the more polished styles of modern jazz. Among the most refined was the
Modern Jazz Quartet. The line-up of
piano, vibraphone, drums, and bass produced a cool, clear-cut display of skilful
technique and improvisation. This was
music for concentrated listening.

Some jazz today is 'free form' improvisation without any rules whatsoever!

Meanwhile the European tradition of
opera continued as the American Broad-
way musicals. These were spectacularly
staged love stories, with spoken dialogue,
dazzling dance routines, and memorable
melodies. This tradition was largely due to
Jewish immigrants from eastern Europe.
The first of these was Irving Berlin (1888-
1989). He came to America from Russia as

Leonard Bernstein was a charismatic showman whose talents ranged from classical to popular composition. His best known work is the music for *West Side Story*.

a baby, and began his long career as a bar-room pianist. He wrote 'God Bless America', 'White Christmas', and many musicals including *Annie Get Your Gun*.

George Gershwin (1898-1937) mixed jazz and European music, and his *Rhapsody in Blue* is a blend of Negro blues and European romantic piano concerto. His opera *Porgy and Bess* is European in construction, but the cast is black and the singing style is jazz. Gershwin also wrote a number of musicals.

Rodgers and Hammerstein wrote *The Sound of Music* — perhaps the best known of all musicals.

Leonard Bernstein (1918-90) was particularly versatile. He was a great showman, conductor, and orchestral composer. His best-known work is the musical, *West Side Story*. The words are by Stephen Sondheim (born 1930), now the greatest American writer of musicals.

In the 1930s Hollywood became the world's film centre. This led to a great demand for composers. Among the greatest of these are Dmitri Tiomkin (1899-1979), and Miklós Rózsa (born 1907) who specialized in large-scale epics like *Ben Hur* and *El Cid*. Film music is essentially romantic in style.

In 300 years America has produced a completely new musical culture of its own, made up of the traditions of many European and African nations.

8

The twentieth century

Our century is an age of experimentation. It opened with gigantic sounds of late romanticism, hazy impressionism, and atonal serialism.

Atonality (without tonality) is the most important feature of twentieth-century music. It rejects traditional rules for melody, rhythm, and harmony. Composers are free to make up their own rules about what fits and what does not. Atonal music sounds discordant, and needs concentrated listening.

Because of radio and recording, the twentieth century has produced a variety of music unimaginable in Mozart's day: in jazz, rock, and pop, as well as classical, styles have changed as quickly as fashion.

Six French composers, together known as *Les Six*, aimed to make music less atonal, shorter and tighter, with some innovative harmonies. The ballet *Le Boeuf sur le Toit* (The Ox on the Roof), by Darius Milhaud (1892-1974) is 'fun' music, full of rollicking Brazilian and jazz rhythms. Arthur Honegger (1892-1955) is remembered for his *Pacific 231*, a musical portrait of an American train.

The 1917 Revolution influenced music in Russia. Igor Stravinsky (1882-1971) experimented with unusual harmonies and

Igor Stravinsky. His ballet, *The Rite of Spring*, was so revolutionary in style that the audience actually rioted at its first performance.

rhythms, but his new atonal ideas were misunderstood. His ballet *The Rite of Spring* caused a riot at its first performance. Sergei Prokofiev (1891-1953), who wrote the children's musical tale *Peter and the Wolf*, was a great ballet composer. Dmitri Shostakovitch (1906-1975) wrote fifteen symphonies, including the sombre 'Leningrad' Symphony composed during

the German siege of that city, now called St Petersburg. He wrote many film scores.

In communist Russia composers had to write 'politically correct' music, including trite tunes, boisterous marches for the working classes, and descriptions of factories. Alexander Mossolov (1900-73), wrote the noisy orchestral *Iron Foundry*. The Russian leader Stalin hated it, and as a punishment Mossolov was sent to Siberia to collect folk tunes!

Prokofiev and Shostakovitch were also in trouble with Stalin for writing 'middle class' music. Shostakovitch was banned because Stalin disliked his Fourth Symphony. He wrote a fifth symphony, entitled *A Soviet Artist's Reply to Just Criticism*. Stalin liked it and allowed him to continue composing.

In Hungary Béla Bartók (1881-1945) was fascinated by the irregular rhythms and strange melodies of Hungarian, Romanian, and Slovak folk tunes. He collected 8000, and arranged many in modern style. This included playing slightly out of tune, using curious modes and harmonies, and constantly changing time signatures.

Bartók's *Mikrokosmos* is a collection of piano pieces designed as a teaching method, progressing from very easy to extremely difficult.

Bartók's fellow Hungarian, Zoltan Kodály (1882-1967), also used folk music for inspiration. His *Hary Janos*, a musical portrayal of a storyteller describing Napoleon's wars, opens with an orchestral sneeze!

In England, romanticism continued with Sir Ralph Vaughan Williams (1872-1958) and Sir Edward Elgar (1857-1934), whose *Pomp and Circumstance March No 1* con-

▲ **The Russian composer Shostakovitch worked under the shadow of communism. Stalin banned his music for ten years because he objected to his Fourth Symphony.**

Elgar's music, of which the Pomp and Circumstance March and 'Enigma Variations' are the best known, was England's most patriotic composer this century.

tains the famous 'Land of Hope and Glory'. Gustav Holst (1874-1934) wrote the 'Planets' Suite.

The musicals of Andrew Lloyd Webber (born 1948) combine romantic harmonies, the opera tradition, and rock music. Among his works are *Joseph and the Amazing Technicolour Dreamcoat*, *Jesus Christ Superstar*, and *Phantom of the Opera*.

Modern atonal ideas came with Sir Michael Tippett (born 1905), composer of the opera *A Child of Our Time*. The greatest British composer was Benjamin Britten (1913-76). His operas such as *Peter Grimes* are very popular. He has written a great deal for children, including the *Young Person's Guide to the Orchestra*. His atonal music is easy to listen to.

The Frenchman Olivier Messiaen (born 1908) is a religious mystic whose strange and complex music seems to reach for the stars. His best known work is the massive 'Turangalila' Symphony, possibly the first 'psychedelic' music ever written. The ten movements have cosmic names, such as 'Garden of Love's Sleep' and 'Joy of the Blood of the Stars'. It is scored for a big orchestra with an enormous array of percussion instruments. It features the first ever keyboard synthesiser, invented in 1928, the ondes martenot (pronounced ornd martin-oh).

Messiaen was imprisoned by the Nazis in a concentration camp, where he wrote *Quartet for the End of Time* for performance by his fellow prisoners.

In Germany, Carl Orff (1895-1982) founded a teaching method for schools. His popular setting of mediaeval Latin poetry, *Carmina Burana*, uses startling and exciting contrasts of instruments and massed voices. Kurt Weill (1900-50) wrote *The Threepenny Opera*, a musical which uses jazz themes. He fled to America to escape the Nazis.

Nazism and communism caused many other composers to flee to the USA. Among them was the Czech Bohuslav Martinů (1890-1959), Stravinsky, Schoenberg, and Bartók.

9

Odyssey into the twenty-first century

The second half of the twentieth century produced even more strange ideas. A lot of music was now completely atonal.

The Pole Krzysztof Penderecki (born 1933) and the Hungarian György Ligeti (born 1923) were writing big 'blocks' of sound with no rhythm, melody, or harmony; not so much music as musical sound effects. Even the notation for this music is different. Ligeti's 'Requiem' was used in the film *2001: A Space Odyssey*.

The atonal music of Glasgow-born Oliver Knussen (born 1952) needs concentrated listening. His opera about monsters, *Where the Wild Things Are*, is frequently performed on television.

The twentieth century has produced new concepts. In Russia Alexander Scriabin (1872-1915) scored his *Prometheus*, describing the God of Fire, for orchestra and an organ which played coloured lights! The idea was considered crazy at the time, and did not work; but in today's rock music, light shows and videos are common. Jean Michel Jarre's 'Synthesiser' concerts include spectacular laser shows.

▶ *Where the Wild Things Are*, **a picture book for children, inspired a popular television opera by the Scottish composer Oliver Knussen.**

There were experiments with the human voice. Schoenberg's *Pierrot Lunaire* is a set of poems set to music, and scored for an unusual combination of instruments. The female voice speaks the words in a musical way. This is called Sprachgesang (in German, *Sprach* means speak and *Gesang* means song).

England's Sir William Walton (1902-1983), wrote film music, and also the 'Facade' Suite, a collection of whimsical pieces with Edith Sitwell's poems spoken over it. It was turned into a ballet. Cathy Berberian (born 1933), wife of atonal composer Pierre Boulez (born 1925), uses her mouth in every way, to sing, to shout, make noises, and click her tongue.

In rock music, rap consists of words spoken over a drum beat.

The American John Cage (born 1912),

It takes a genius or a joker to compose for 12 radios tuned to different stations, as did John Cage pictured here.

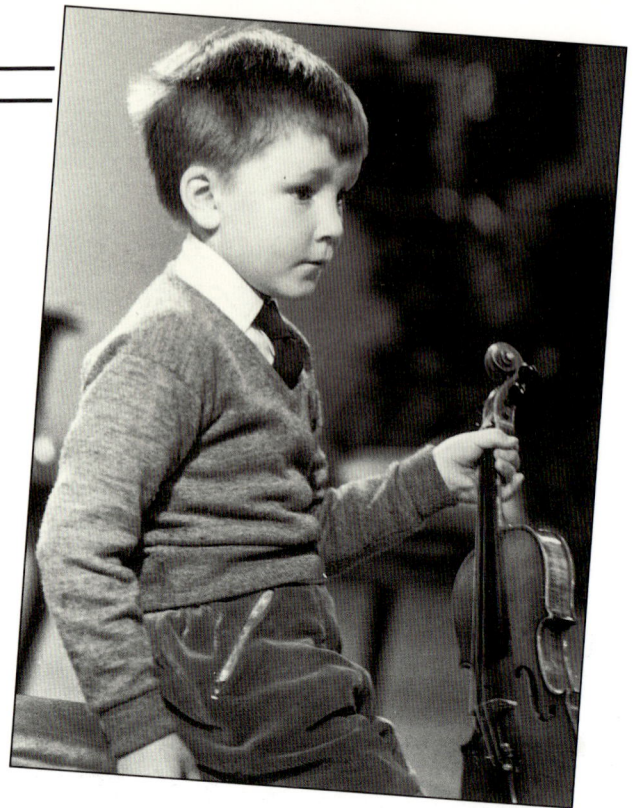

Violinist Nigel Kennedy's talent was recognised at an early age. This photograph shows him as a little boy attending a Yehudi Menuhin Masterclass.

pupil of Schoenberg, composed *4 minutes 33 seconds*. The pianist sits at the piano in total silence for that time! He also uses a 'prepared piano', with bolts and screws between the strings for extra percussive effects. Some prepared pianos were re-tuned to quarter-tones, or half-semitones, making them sound out of tune, and similar to Gamelan orchestras.

Estonian Arvo Pärt (born 1935) and Henryk Górecki (born 1933) of Poland, whose hauntingly beautiful Third Symphony is one of the century's most popular works, have rejected atonal music in favour of plainchant and medieval polyphony.

Electronics also played a part. Radio signals, bleeps, and squeaks, as well as natural sounds like traffic, birds, and machines, were recorded and re-arranged by being slowed down, sped up, played backwards, and tampered with in every way. This was called 'Musique Concrète'. One example is the theme to television's *Dr Who* series, constructed by the BBC Radiophonic workshop out of radio noises.

Tape recorders are used in some performances. The German Karlheinz Stockhausen (born 1928) uses pre-recorded tapes together with live musicians.

In rock music, many keyboard synthesiser players also 'prepare' their instruments using built-in computers to produce special effects at the flick of a switch.

A lot of atonal music is left to chance. Musicians are given instructions which they carry out in their own time. No one knows how it will turn out.

The same can perhaps be said of the twenty-first century!

10

Music from around the world

African music

Music is an important part of the tribal life of Africans, who have a natural gift for music and rhythm. Births, deaths, marriage, sickness, initiation, and fertility rites are celebrated in song and dance. Work chants accompany anything from pounding grain to paddling canoes. The music, always harmonized, is traditional in pattern, and often improvised. It is handed down from generation to generation by ear.

African music crossed the Atlantic in slave ships during the seventeenth and eighteenth centuries. It merged with European music and built the foundations of American music, as we have shown in Chapter 7.

◀ **African dancing – as shown in this picture of a traditional Zulu war dance – is today used on ceremonial occasions and festivals. The inspiration for jazz, rock and pop music can be traced back to the rhythms and harmonies of Africa.**

⬆ **Gipsy music, full of dash and rhythm, is always associated with dancing. In this painting a gipsy girl dances with a tambourine.**

important role in Chinese theatre, a colourful mixture of singing, playing, poetry, acting, dancing, mime and acrobatics. The traditional orchestra consists of about eight instruments, including the koto (a type of zither), and sets the scene. The Peking Opera is world famous for its highly stylized performances.

Chinese music uses the pentatonic scale.

Gipsy music

The gipsies are nomads who came to Europe from northern India, bringing two musical styles. The first is the flamenco music of Spain. The gipsies who settled there adopted the guitar and developed a spectacular style of singing and dancing. It features tap dancing to complicated rhythms and playing castanets.

The second group settled in Hungary and Romania, where they adopted European instruments, especially the violin. The most common music is the csardas (pronounced chardash). A band will have two violins, a double bass, a cymbalom (a zither with strings struck with hammers), and a clarinet. A csardas begins slowly, then bursts into breakneck speed. The musicians will each show off their skills. Gipsy bands play at weddings and village dances.

Flamenco and csardas are exciting, and the music and dance develop into a frenzy. Showing off is an essential ingredient.

Arabic music

Arabic music developed in the home, and there is little tradition of public performance. The Islamic religion does not encourage music, and some religious leaders oppose it as a distraction from worship.

The guitar and the lute are Arabic in origin, and were brought to Spain by the Moors in the Middle Ages. The complex rhythms and instruments were absorbed into European music.

Indian music

Classical Indian music consists of complex melodies and rhythms, usually played on sitar and tablas. The musical form is the

Chinese music

Chinese music, graceful and delicate, originated as temple worship. It plays an raga. The sitar first plays the scale to be used. Then the melody is played and developed. The sitar player and tabla player together 'create' the raga, which increases in speed and complexity. Ragas are improvised within a strict framework. Much skill and creativity are required to master these two difficult instruments. Ragas are performed at specific times of day.

In the nineteenth century the British imported the harmonium — a bellows-operated organ. Today the portable version is the most popular Indian instrument.

Indian dancing is performed to an accompaniment of bells and drums. It is very formal and often tells a story.

Indonesian Gamelan music

A Gamelan orchestra consists of tuned percussion instruments, such as xylophones, marimbas, and gongs, as well as drums. As these instruments are tuned to an Indonesian scale of five notes, Gamelan music sounds 'out of tune' to those unfamiliar with it. A Gamelan orchestra can have thirty players.

Gamelans also accompany Javanese temple dancing, which is done by girls trained from childhood. The formal and ritualistic dance tells a story and the movements are strictly laid down. The expressive hand movements are a form of language, and every angle of the body must be exactly correct.

Japanese music

Traditional Japanese music uses ideas not used anywhere else and may sound strange to those not used to it. Sometimes the gap between one note and the next is full of meaning. Instruments such as the koto (a type of zither designed like a dragon's back), the biwa (a bass lute), and the shakuhachi (a long, bamboo flute) are a feature.

The most famous Indian musician is sitar player Ravi Shankar (left). Here he is accompanied by tabla (hand drums) and tanpura (droning strings).

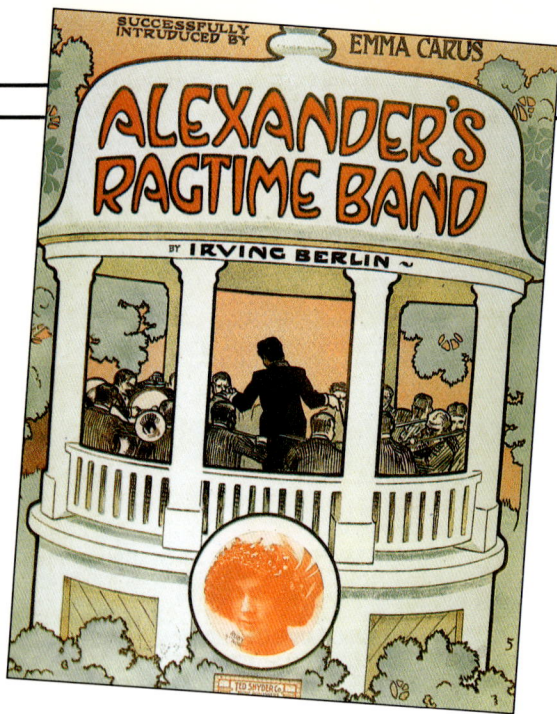

Irving Berlin, who wrote 'Alexander's Ragtime Band' while working as a singing waiter, helped to shape 20th-century American music.

Modern Japan has taken to European music in a big way. Some of the world's finest performers of Western music are Japanese. The famous Suzuki teaching method is used world-wide.

Jewish music

The Bible mentions psalteries (a type of zither), cornets (a primitive oboe), harps, cymbals, and trumpets, for celebration and dancing in ancient Israel. God was praised in song. In today's synagogues sung music is an important part of the ceremonies, and the cantor is expected to be a fine singer.

There is a wealth of Jewish folk music, rhythmic and usually in the minor key, which gives it a distinctly melancholy feel. The traditional dance is the hora. The participants form a circle with arms round each other's shoulders, and dance round as the music gets faster.

Jewish folk music has influenced music wherever Jews have settled, especially in Russia and eastern Europe, where Yiddish 'Klezmer' bands, invariably featuring a clarinet virtuoso, are often heard at weddings and barmitzvah ceremonies.

In the USA, Jewish musicians such as George Gershwin, Irving Berlin, and Leonard Bernstein have helped create modern American music, as we have shown in Chapter 7.

Latin-American music

Latin-American music is a mixture of romantic Spanish, Portuguese, and Italian songs, and African rhythm. Mexican street bands feature trumpets and guitars. Latin-American bands use maracas, bongoes, conga drums, claves — and a donkey's jaw — to produce the exciting rhythms of the Cuban rumba, the Brazilian samba, the mambo, and cha-cha-cha. Typical instruments are guitars made from turtle shells, pan pipes, and small Paraguayan harps.

The Brazilian composer Heitor Villa-Lobos (1887-1959) combined exotic samba rhythms with European classical music. His *Little Train of Caipira* describes a Brazilian steam engine puffing and clanking through the jungle.

The tango, an Argentine dance whose strong, passionate beat conquered Europe in the 1920s, is played by a band consisting of a bandoleon (a type of concertina), violin, piano, guitar, and double bass.

The West Indian calypso, where clever words are improvised to music, is the forerunner of rap. Reggae, the music of the Jamaican Rastafarians, is recognized by its chunky, off-beat rhythm. Its greatest exponent was Bob Marley (1945-80).

⬆ **To the Maoris singing in harmony comes naturally. In a group like this there may be as many harmonies as there are singers.**

North American Indian music

Dancing featured in American Indian ceremonies and entertainment. They were performed round totem poles to drums, rattles, and reed pipes, often lasting for several days. They were used before hunting expeditions, seed planting, initiations of young braves, and for whipping up war frenzy. Music had a magical significance. Songs were used as incantations against illnesses, supplications to the spirits, and recounting legends. Melodies were no more than chants. There was no harmony, and the pentatonic scale was generally used.

American Indian music is now virtually extinct, and replaced by the Afro-European tradition.

Polynesian music

The relaxed music of the South Seas owes much to Portuguese seafarers who introduced the guitar. This led to the smaller version, the warm-toned ukelele, used to accompany songs and chants. The twentieth century brought the electric Hawaiian guitar. It is placed on a table, and played with a plectrum in the right hand and a small steel bar in the left, so the player can slide from one note to the other.

This slurring of notes is a feature of Polynesian music. It accompanied the swaying hula hula dancers wearing garlands of flowers and grass skirts. The Hawaiian guitar was adopted in the USA by country and western bands, and is called the steel guitar.

Among the finest singers in the South Seas are the Maoris, the original inhabitants of New Zealand, who are renowned for beautiful harmony singing.

Scales and modes

Ancient Chinese names

Pentatonic scale

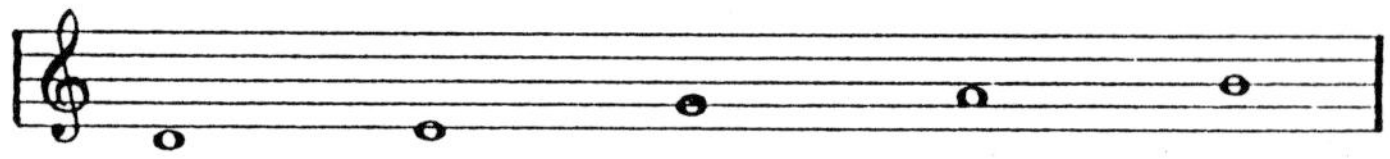
Affairs of state
Mirror of the world
Emperor
Prime minister
Loyal subjects

Dorian mode

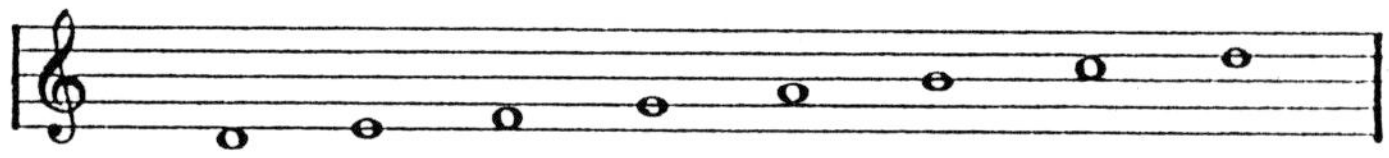

Phrygian mode

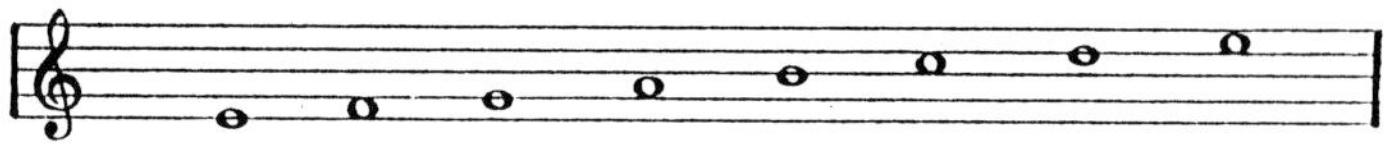

Lydian mode

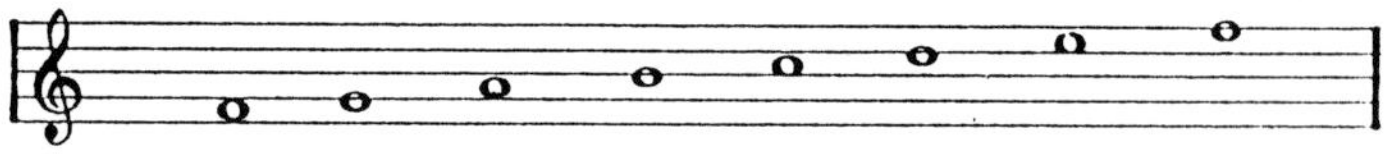

Mixolydian mode

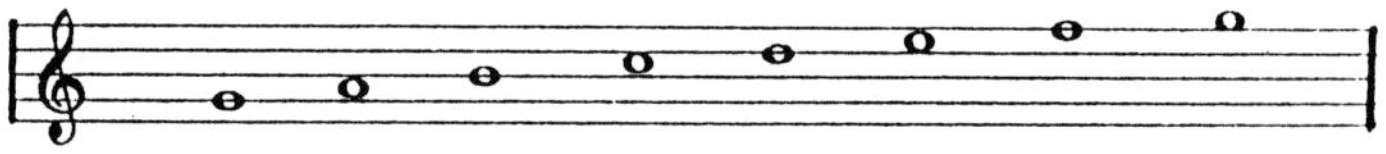

Aeolian mode

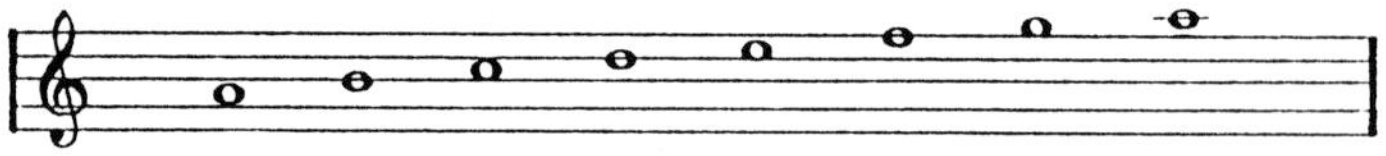

Ionic mode, or Diatonic major scale

Sol-fa names

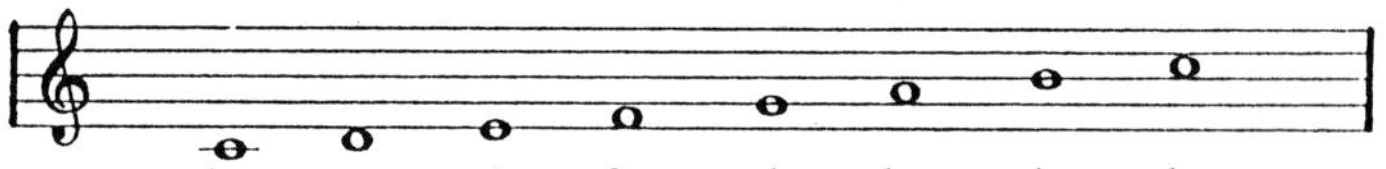
do
re
mi
fa
soh
la
ti
do

Scale degree names

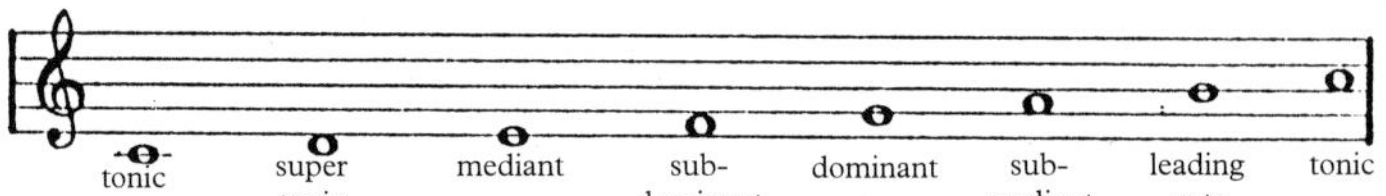
tonic
super tonic
mediant
sub-dominant
dominant
sub-mediant
leading note
tonic

Harmonic minor scale

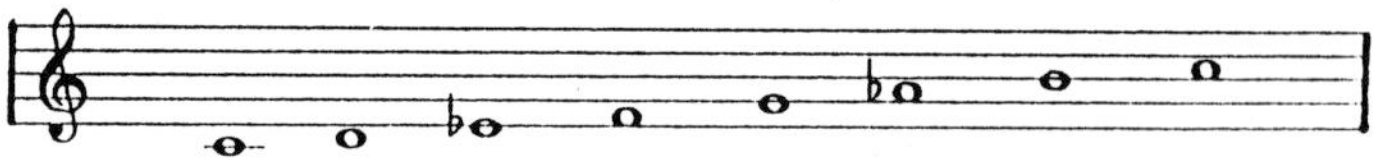

Melodic minor scale

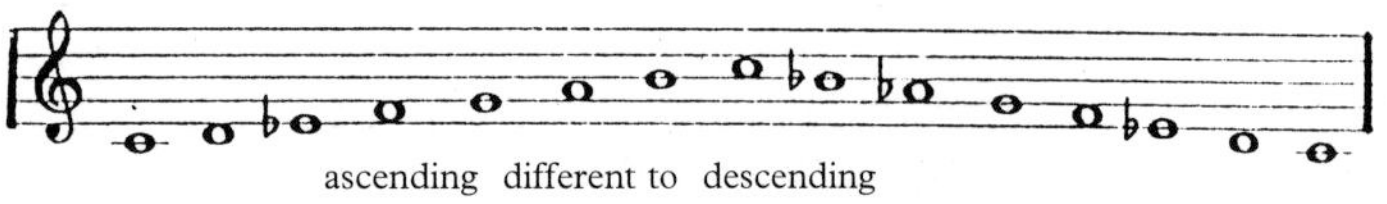
ascending different to descending

Chromatic scale

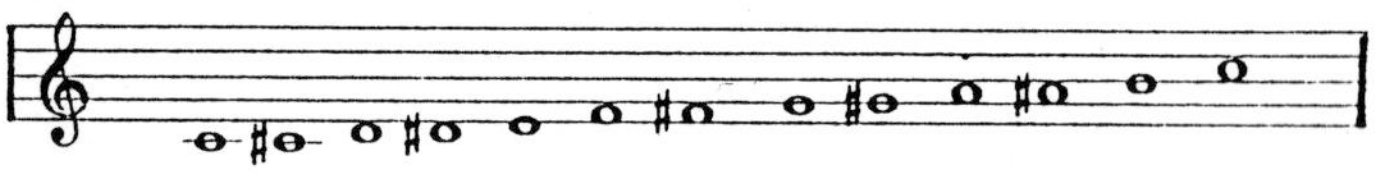

Whole-tone scale

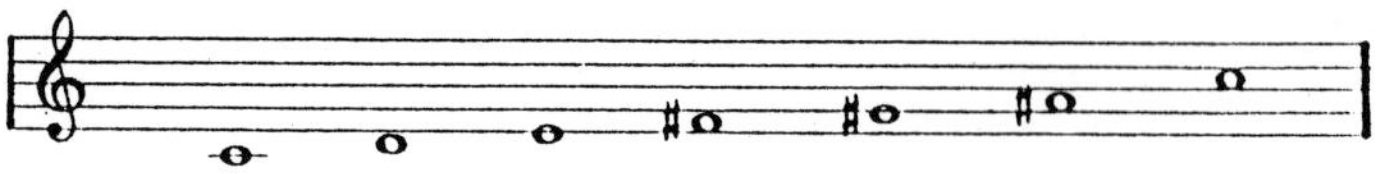

Glossary

aria: one of the main solo songs in an opera or oratorio.

atonality: discordant music which does not obey the rules of harmony.

ballad: a song which tells a story of love, romance, or adventure.

beat: the strong notes, the ones you tap your foot to.

chord: two or more notes that fit together to make harmony.

classical: the music of the seventeenth and eighteenth centuries (as opposed to romantic or impressionist music, or any other style). Another meaning of the word is all 'serious' music which is not pop, rock, jazz, etc.

clavier: German for 'keyboard'. Until the nineteenth century all domestic keyboard instruments, including harpsichords and pianos, were called claviers.

concerto: a piece of music, usually divided into three movements, for a solo instrument backed by an orchestra. Some concertos feature groups of two, three, or even four instruments.

harmony: the pleasing sound made by notes fitting together.

improvisation: composing music at the same time as you play it - making it up as you go.

key: the pitch of a piece of music, based around a main note called the keynote. This keynote could be any note in the scale. If a song is difficult to sing because the pitch is too high, the key can be lowered to any other keynote of the scale.

key: another meaning of key is the lever on a musical instrument which is pressed to vary a note.

mass: the religious ceremony celebrating the Last Supper. The ceremony is often set to music, with parts of it sung, and this is also called a mass.

melody: a string of notes arranged to make a pleasing tune.

modes: the various ancient systems of scales used before modern scales were established (see Scales and modes on page 46).

movement: the separate parts into which symphonies, concertos, and suites are divided.

notation: a way of representing the sounds of music in written form.

note: one musical sound.

octave: the eight notes of a scale.

opera: a play whose words are sung all the way through.

oratorio: a Bible story set to music, for solo voices, chorus and orchestra. Unlike opera, there is no acting.

pitch: the 'highness' or 'lowness' of a sound.

polyphony: more than one tune being played at the same time.

quartet: four players, or a piece of music written for four players.

rhythm: the regular pattern of strong and weak beats in a piece of music.

scale: a series of notes arranged in a particular order.

score: the musical parts of a composition written out in full. It includes every instrument and every voice.

semitone: half a tone.

signature: the signs put at the beginning of a piece of music to show the key and the time.

stave: the system of five lines on which music is written; also called a staff.

symphony: a large-scale orchestral composition, usually divided into four movements.

tone: the interval, or distance, from one note to the next (for example from C to D).

trill: two notes, next to each other, played alternately at great speed.

tune: a string of notes to be played or sung. Another meaning of the word is to adjust the pitch of an instrument so that it plays the exact note.

Index

Works mentioned
(a selection)